We Ain't Kids Anymore

Ceazia Barr

Published by Ceazia Barr, 2025.

While every precaution has been taken in the preparation of this book, the publisher assumes no responsibility for errors or omissions, or for damages resulting from the use of the information contained herein.

WE AIN'T KIDS ANYMORE

First edition. January 15, 2025.

Copyright © 2025 Ceazia Barr.

ISBN: 979-8230053613

Written by Ceazia Barr.

To Aaron , My Boyfriend and My Mom, Desiree

The room is quiet
But my mind is loud
A thousand voices shouting
When i need just one sound

                                      The sun rises
                                      But i don't
                          Its warmth never reaches
                          The cold beneath my skin

We spoke in whispers,
Afraid of the truth.
Now silence remains,
Where love once grew

                                  The phone doesn't ring,
                              But i don't know who id call
                                        Empty hands,
                                Holding nothing at all

I stay behind the glass ,
Watching the world move
Not alone ,
But not seen

                I take a step forward but chains pull me back .
                            I move through the day ,
                                  A ghost , a shadow
                                    Not fully here,
                                When i was a kid
              I used to think being a teenager would be fun
                              It some ways it is
                                  In some its not
                              But all i know is
                       I want to be a kid again .

"Hold my hand until we turn to ashes

Love me til they put me in my casket
I got all these feelings that im masking"

    - The kid laroi

                    ""We didnt give a fuck back then
                              I aint a kid no more"
                                    - Frank Ocean

And when you held me
It felt like i was
Finally safe

                            She thought i was trouble
                              But i was just trying
                                To figure it all out

My mom used to tell me
During a breakup
Ask yourself
"What are you really losing?"

                                      I hate mean girls

You were so toxic
That i began to believe
It was all my fault

                        I loved you with all my heart
                                        I still do
                But i eventually have to move on

"Everything sucked back then"

                          I would let ugly people
                                          Ruin
                    The prettiest pieces of me

I knew our relationship
Wasn't worth it
When the people closest
To me questioned

WE AIN'T KIDS ANYMORE

Why i was even still
With you

                    You cheated , lied , made me so insecure
                        And a part of me still believes
                          That you actually loved me

All i can do is look back
And be grateful
That i'm not in that
Situation anymore

                " i care for you still and i will forever"
                      White Ferrari Frank Ocean

I feel like such a fool
Because people warned me
And i saw the red flags
But i felt like i was
And exception

                            You kept me a secret
                                For so long
                        That i didn't even know
                            I existed to you

Music heals what
Other people break
And so does poetry

                      "I just wanna runaway
              But all i ever do is run in place"
                          "Ruby Da Cherry"

"If you could die
And come back to life
Up for the air from the swimming pool
You'd kneel down to the dry land
Kiss the earth that birthed you

Gave you tools just stay alive"
-Frank Ocean

                                            Sometimes and wonder
                                               What version of me
                                         People have in their heads

The skys so blue,
It's kind of sweet to think about you,
But now i'm in another life,
Pretending it's paradise

                                            We're not kids anymore,
                                                I can't make you stay.
                                             I thought I was dreaming.
                                    When you said goodbye that day

If i'm in love with you
Why am i so alone?/
You keep my head above water,
But your hands are still gone

                                                 Summertimes magic,
                                          But I'm cold in its glow.
                             You're running through my mind,
                                       And i can't let you go

I'll be your satellite
Orbiting what we lost.
I hope you find your heaven
No matter what it costs

                                                  I miss the feeling,
                                   Of mornings spent with you.
                                     It's just a memory now,
                                       But it feels so true

You're so misunderstood,
Yet you carry the blame.
In another life,

WE AIN'T KIDS ANYMORE

Id call your name

                      I gave you something real,
                      But you threw it all away.
                      Now i'm a silhouette,
                      Fading with the day

Be yourself , they said,
But I don't know who I am.
I keep losing pisces,
Like footprints in the sand

                      We were too fast ,
                      But it felt like fate.
                      Now i'm staring at the clock,
                      As love turns to hate

I swam too far,
Chasing dreams in the dark.
You were my lighthouse,
But now there's no spark

                      I'll be your hero,
                      Even when I'm alone.
                      Cause every story needs a savior,
                      And i'm better on my own

The nights feel endless,
And your voice feels near.
Even in my dreams
I can't escape the fear

                      But if it's forever it's even better

You call me crazy,
But you're the reason why.
I follow you through the dark,
Chasing your goodbye

                      Summer air,
                      The taste of youth.

>   We ran too fast,
>   Searching for the truth

I said too much
You said too little.
We're a love story,
Stuck in the middle

>   You're my wish,
>   The one I seek.
>   But wishes crumble,
>   When hearts are weak.

I hate your guts
But i love your smile
You're the poison to my heart
But i'd stay awhile

>   You're the call i make
>   At 3am
>   When the world feels small

The sky is endless, blue and wide,
But my heart feels small tonight.
Your love was summer, soft and fleeting,
Now it's winter, my heart still beating.
>   You kissed me once under the neon glow,
>   But promises fade, like stars in the snow.
>   Your hands were warm, but your words were cold,
>   A story unfinished, a tale untold.
We danced to the sound of a broken tune,
Under a blood-red, crying moon.
California dreams, soft and sweet,
Turned to ashes beneath my feet.
>   You were my church, my holy sin,
>   But even gods fall from within.

WE AIN'T KIDS ANYMORE

> I drove too far, chasing your name,
> But the road disappeared; it's never the same.
> You tasted like freedom, wild and untamed,
> But freedom fades when hearts are maimed.

I wore my red dress, hoping you'd see,
But you only loved the idea of me.
Venice Beach sunsets, lovers and lies,
We burned too bright, then said our goodbyes.

> Your voice was a hymn, a gentle prayer,
> Now it's silent, lingering in the air.
> Golden days and cigarette haze,
> Your love was on fire, but it couldn't stay.

I chased your shadow through desert storms,
But shadows disappear when the sun warms.
Your name still lingers, soft on my tongue,
Like a tragic ballad, forever sung.

> I painted my heart with shades of you,
> But the colors faded, now only blue.
> Your love was a flame, wild and free,
> Now it's just smoke choking me.

We drove past the ocean, hearts alight,
But love got lost in the dead of night.
You loved the idea of me, not my soul,
Now I'm just trying to feel whole.

> I wore flowers in my hair for you,
> But you loved thorns, and the damage grew.
> I stood at the edge, waiting for your call,
> But the silence answered, louder than it all.

We made promises under pale moonlight,
But promises fade with the morning light.
I sang for you, soft and sweet,
But the melody broke, left incomplete.

> Your love was champagne, sweet and bright,
> But the glass shattered on a lonely night.
> I wore your jacket, it smelled like sin,

But even sins have an ending within.
We lived like rebels, hearts on fire,
But every flame dies when it burns too high.

> I wrote your name on the back of my hand,
> But the ink smudged, a love unplanned.
> We danced to the sound of a broken heart,
> But every dance ends, and we fell apart.

The roses you gave me have long since died,
But their thorns remain, deep inside.
You were my America, wild and free,
But even empires fall into the sea.

> I sang for love, and it sang for me,
> But the harmony broke in tragedy.
> Your lips tasted like a bittersweet dream,
> But dreams dissolve in the morning stream.
> We stood in the rain, hearts exposed,

But love was a book that never closed.
I wore my pearls for you to see,
But you only loved the mystery.

> The freeway lights blurred, tears in my eyes,
> Love was a movie, but it ended in lies.
> We kissed beneath the Hollywood sign,
> But fame and love don't intertwine.

Your voice was a lullaby, soft and sweet,
But the song faded in bittersweet defeat.
We drove to the coast, hearts in bloom,
But the tide pulled us apart too soon.
Your love was a castle, grand and tall,
But castles crumble, and empires fall.

WE AIN'T KIDS ANYMORE

You said forever, but forever died,
Now I wear your promises like chains inside.
You were the dream, the fire, the sea,
But dreams and fires consume me.
I wore my heart on a diamond chain,
But diamonds break, leaving only pain.

We wrote our names in the sand that night,
But the ocean claimed them before the light.

Your love was an ocean, vast and deep,
But the waves crashed, leaving me to weep.

We kissed in the dark, no promises made,
But love fades fast in the shade.

You gave me your heart, fragile and thin,
But hearts can't hold where lies begin.

I'm just tryna stay sane,
Caught in the web of this game.

Woke up, hope's gone,
World moving, but I'm still stuck in dawn.

Fast life, fast cars,
Dreams of shooting for the stars.

Life feels like a black hole,
Can't escape, I'm losing control.

I'm reaching for a vision,
But the pain's my prison.

Every step, the world's a puzzle,
In this storm, I try not to hustle.

I'm torn between peace and pain,
In the chaos, I remain.

Whispers in my ear,
Telling me to fight or disappear.

Heart heavy, mind's lost,
In this battle, I pay the cost.

Living like it's all a race,
Caught up in the chase for grace.

Thoughts are loud, can't hear a thing,
I'm on the edge, about to spring.

Trying to find myself in the maze,
But the world keeps me in a daze.

Love feels distant, it's a lie,
But I keep reaching for the sky.

Running through the dark,
I'm searching for a spark.

Can't trust the silence,
It screams louder than my defiance.

I wear my pain like a crown,
But inside, I'm slowly breaking down.

Told myself to keep going,
Even when the winds kept blowing.

Streets speak, but I'm not listening,
Trying to find peace, but I'm still missing.

Time ticks, but I'm still behind,
Chasing a piece of peace I can't find.

Fighting demons in my sleep,
But I'm awake, drowning deep.

Life's a puzzle with missing parts,
I search for answers in broken hearts.

I'm living for the highs and lows,
But sometimes, I'm just frozen in the lows.

I drown in my own thoughts,
But still, I fight for what I've sought.

Eyes closed, but I still see,
The weight of what they expect from me.

The world's loud, my soul's quiet,
I'm drowning in a riot.

WE AIN'T KIDS ANYMORE

> I dream of freedom, but I'm caged,
> Fighting battles, feeling enraged.
> Every day's a new war,
> But I keep fighting for something more.

They try to break me, but I stand,
In the storm, I make my stand.

> Every scar's a lesson learned,
> But in this world, I still feel burned.

Hiding pain in my smile,
But it takes more to heal in style.

> Caught in a storm of doubt,
> But I'll figure it out, no doubt.

Racing against the clock,
But time always seems to mock.

> I'm chasing dreams, but they're running,
> My heart's heavy, my soul's stunning.

Pressure builds, cracks start to show,
But I'll never let the pain grow.

> Lost in thoughts, can't get out,
> But still, I try without a doubt.

Living life like a movie,
But it's a tragedy, not a comedy.

> Heart full of passion, mind full of pain,
> But I keep walking in the rain.

Torn between fate and free will,
I keep climbing, I keep still.

> Beneath the stars, I search for truth,
> But I'm stuck in the trap of my youth.

Hoping for better days,
But tomorrow's still a haze.

> I'm trapped in my own design,
> But somehow, I still shine.

I feel the weight of the world,
But still, I keep my vision unfurled.
    Shadows follow, but I keep running,
    The sun's setting, but I'm still stunning.
Voices echo in my mind,
But peace is something I can't find.
    The struggle's real, but I stay strong,
    In this world, I've been wronged too long.
Trapped in a dream, can't wake up,
But still, I fill my cup.
    The noise outside keeps growing,
    But in silence, I keep knowing.
I keep fighting even when I fall,
Because the pain makes me stand tall.
    Thoughts like fire, burn inside,
    But I'll keep moving, no place to hide.
In the darkness, I find my way,
Hoping that light will shine one day.
    Every breath feels like a race,
    But I'm still chasing that embrace.
I'm moving, but I'm stuck,
Trying to get out of this muck.
    Every dream feels out of reach,
    But I'll keep fighting, I'll never breach.
Life's a blur, but I see through,
Chasing peace in everything I do.
    Through the pain, I find the key,
    The truth lies deep inside of me.
Waking up, but I'm still asleep,
In this world, I'm sinking deep.
    Hope is the only thing that heals,
    But it's a struggle to see how it feels.

WE AIN'T KIDS ANYMORE

I try to fly but feel the ground,
But still, I rise above the sound.

                              I sleep so i can see you
                                    Because i hate
                                        To wait so long

But nothing can capture the sting
Of the venom she's gonna spit
Out right now

                              I thought i was dreaming
                                  When you said
                                      You loved me

Its ok to hate me
But we both know deep down
The feelings still good

                          We had time to kill back then

You aint a kid anymore

                          I had no chance to prepare
                          Couldn't see you coming

Its bad luck to talk
On these ride

                              Sweet 16 how was i
                        Supposed to know anything

I didn't care
To state the plain

                            We're so both familiar
                                Good times

Mind over matter is magic
I do magic

                                      In this life
                                      In this life

Im sure we're taller
In another dimension

                                    You saye we're small
                                    And not worth the mention
Clearly this isn't.
                                    Cant take whats been given
                                    But we're so okay here
                                    We're doing fine
Primal and naked
You dream of walls that hold us in prison
                                    I got all these feelings
                                    That i'm maskin
I think about you
And nothing else
                        It's nights like this when i need your love
                        When i need someone that'll heal my soul
Fallen star
I'm your one call away
                                    Motel halls neon walls
                                    When night falls
                                    I am your escape.
If you've been waiting
For fallin in love
Babe you don't have
To wait on me
                                    Cus what you want
                                    Is what i want
                                    Sincerity
Souls that dream
Alone lie awake
I'll give you something
So real
                                    Pull me oh so close
                                    Cuz you never know

WE AIN'T KIDS ANYMORE

                        How long our lives will
                                    be.

Cus i been aiming for heaven
Above but an angel
Ain't what i need

                    That's the way everyday goes
                    Everytime we have no control

If you could fly
Then you'd feel south

                          You showed me love
                          Glory from above
                          Regard my dear

In the wake of a hurricane
Dark Skin of a summer shade
Nosedive in the floodlines

                    Tall tower of milk crates
                It's the same way you showed me

What a life
Remember how it was

                      Gimme something sweet

If that's your ex
You should probably own
A pistol

                  And i just couldn't take it
                  You're so motherfuckin
                      Gorgeous

Check your window He's at your window
                And then he came up to my knees
                    Begging "baby please"
              Could you please do the things
                  You'd say you do to me

Pimpin in my convos

Bubbles in my champagne
Let it be some jazz playing

> You're morning eyes
> I could stare like
> Watching stars

Know you're all i want
In this life
I' ll imagine we
Fell in love

> I'll trust the universe
> Will always bring me back
> To you

I think i'll picture us
You with the waves
The oceans colors
On your face

> I wish i knew you wanted me
> If i knew i'd be with you
> Is it too late to pursue?

Its okay things happen
For reasons i think are sure

> Funny you come back to
> Me my dear

Im everywhere , im cross-eyed
And i can't decide if you're
Invited

> I know i'll be in your heart
> Til the end
> You'll miss me dont beg me
> Babe

Locked in a stalemate
With a man whose bars

WE AIN'T KIDS ANYMORE

No holds

                                        I will always love you
                                                How i do

Wishing you Godspeed, glory
There will be mountains you can't
Move

                              You look down on where you cam
                                        From sometimes
                                        But you'll always
                                      Have this place to
                                            Call home

I'll always love you
Until the time we die

                                          Things fall apart
                                    And time breaks your
                                                    Heart

You fell out of love
And you both let go

                              She was crying on my shoulder
                                All i could do was hold her
                                That only made us closer
                                    Until december

I know that you love me
You don't have to remind me

                                  Put it all behind me
                                  I can still see her
                                  In the back of my
                                          Mind

I know you didn't
Mean to hurt me
So i kept it to
myself

                                        You say no one knows you so well
                                        And everytime you touch me
                                              I wonder how she felt

You got me feeling so
Lonely

                                            Hate the way i love you
                                                  But you're so sweet

Baby come on
Home

                                      I've only recently began to fall
                                  I feel the need to go and waste it all

Watch the sunrise along the
Coast as we're getting old

                                          All i know is we're going
                                    Home so please don't let me go

I don't care how long
It takes as long as im
With you i got a smile on
My face

                                        I wish i could live through
                                              Every memory again

Just one more time before we
Float off in the wind

                                          Waiting for the light to
                                  Take us in has been the greatest
                                              Time of my life

No one tried to read
My eyes
No one but you

                                    Come on , don't leave me bae
                                      It can't be that easy bae

Since you've been gone

WE AIN'T KIDS ANYMORE

I've been having withdrawals

                                                    He asked me
                                            "How to be funny?"
                                  But that's not something you
                                                    Can teach

And i tried to hold him but it didn't last long

                                   How could i miss something
                                              That i never had

I don't want a friend
I want my life

                                      Give me reasons why
                                    We should be complete

I dont fuck with your tone
Can we just go home

                                   You're wasting your tongue
                                   With lame excuses and lies

You don't know how long
I stare into the picture
And wish that it was me

                                            All by yourself
                                            Sittin alone
                                   I hope we're still friends
                                 Yeah i hope you don't mind

I think of him
So much it drives me
Crazy

                                         1 , 2 ,3 and me
                                 1 , 2 Maybe 4 what do i need
                                                You for?

Honestly i belong
With me and only me

                                           What if he's fine?

I just let bad thoughts linger
For just far too long

                                          I think i know
                              I'll touch that fire for you

Long as you're dreamin
About me aint no problems

                                  How can i snooze and
                                      Miss the moment

Let's take this argument b
Back up to my place

                                                I can't lose
                                    When i'm with you

How you blame it on me
And you the main one lying

                          I wish i could live without you
                              But now you're apart of me

Do not enter is written
On the doorway

                        Why can't everyone just go away

I just need someone in
My life to give it structure

                          To handle all the selfish ways i
                              Spend my time without him

I'm gonna pack my things
And leave you behind

                                    This feelings old
And i know that i've made up my mind
                                  I'll never forget you
                  You put me on a feeling i never had

Loving you
is the soft hum of a record spinning,

WE AIN'T KIDS ANYMORE

scratches and all,
a sound that stays long after it stops.

                                    I could write little letters
                                        For you all day long

But all i ever wanted was
To love you in peace

                                          Find peace they say
                                  But how do you find peace
                            When you're living through chaos

"Break up" they say
But we ain't kids no more

                                                  So proud of you
                                      For telling me things
                                      You promised to keep
                                                To yourself

I was full of love back then
But i aint a kid no more
You always told me
How beautiful i am
How you didn't know
How you even got with me
But the truth is
You didn't even
Really have to try
Because i could read
You like a book
And see you were
The one i want to
Pursue life with
You're smile is the most beautiful thing
You think your body is hideous
But God really took his time

On you. In my eyes your so perfect
I just wanna fix the things
You're so insecure about
But you never gave me
The chance to. Because
When i pointed those things
Out . you assumed i was making
Fun of you when i was just trying to
Love you like myself.
my baby,
There's something about the way you exist in this world that feels like magic—effortless and rare. It's like the universe poured its light into you, and somehow, I'm lucky enough to feel its warmth every day.
I can't find the right words to describe how you make me feel, but it's in the little things. like the way your smile is big and bright, or how your touch feels like heaven. It's in the way you make even the smallest moments feel meaningful, like when we would stay up all night and I'd beg you not to go to sleep.
I love how you bring color to my world. the way you pick me up when i'm feeling down or how you always make those corny dad jokes those things remind me how special you are. you make life brighter, softer, and infinitely more beautiful.
you've given me a love that feels like home. in your arms, i feel safe, in your presence, i feel understood. you make me want to be better, to dream bigger, to love deeper. I've never felt so seen, so cared for, so completely myself as I do with you.
Every day with you is a gift. Whether we're laughing at stupid shit or just sitting in comfortable silence, every moment feels like it matters. it's not just what we do—it's that i get to do it with you.
I want you to know that I see you, all of you. your kindness, your strength, your vulnerability, even the pieces of yourself you try to hide I

love it all. You are my favorite story, and I never want to stop turning the pages.

So here I am, putting into words what my heart already knows: you are my always. no matter where life takes us, no matter how far we go, my heart will always be yours.

yours, forever and always,

Ce'azia

---

my love,

I've been thinking a lot lately about the ways I show up in our relationship—the good, the bad, and everything in between. I know that sometimes my emotions can get the better of me, and I let my anger spill over in ways that aren't fair to you. I want you to know that I saw it, and I'm sorry. you deserve the best of me, not the moments when my temper gets in the way.

I also know that I can be needy sometimes, always craving your attention, your reassurance, your presence. It's like I can't get enough of you, and while that comes from the love I feel, I know it can be a lot. I'm sorry if it ever makes you feel overwhelmed or if it feels like I'm asking too much. The truth is, you mean so much to me, and that's why I hold on so tightly. Your love is a light in my life, and sometimes I worry that if I loosen my grip, I might lose it. but i'm learning to trust more—not just in you, but in us. I want to give you the space to breathe, to be yourself, to feel as free in this love as I do.

I'm not perfect, but I'm trying. Every day, I'm trying to be better—not just for you, but for me too. because you deserve someone who loves you in the healthiest, kindest way possible. someone who doesn't just ask for your patience but earns it by growing and learning.

Thank you for loving me through my flaws, for seeing the good in me even when I struggle to see it myself. Thank you for staying, for caring, for being my safe place. Your love means everything to me, and I don't take it for granted.

I promise to keep working on myself, on my temper, and on giving you the freedom to love me in your own way. Because the last thing I want is to make you feel anything less than cherished.

you are my heart, my home, my everything. and for all the ways i fall short, i hope my love makes up for it. because it's real, and it's yours, completely.

forever trying and forever yours,
Ce'azia

---

my love,

I want to start by thanking you. I know that sometimes I'm not the easiest to deal with, but you've shown me nothing but patience, love, and understanding. Even when I feel overwhelmed, you stay by my side, giving me the space I need to breathe and be myself. Your patience means more to me than you'll ever know, and I'll never take it for granted.

I think about the moments we've shared—the ones that have become memories I hold close. like that night at waffle house, when we laughed over hashbrowns and pancakes, talking about everything and nothing. for the first time we went to the park, and I saw how easily you blended into my world, meeting my mom, making me realize just how much you belong here with me. and our first sleepover laying next to you, feeling like time stood still, knowing I never wanted it to end.

you've always known how to make me feel special, even in the simplest ways. like when you stay up late with me, sending me songs that remind you of me, or sharing funny videos that make me smile no matter how tough the day has been. when you play my favorite video games with me, or when you try something new just to make me happy, it's like you're telling me, without words, that you see me. and that means the world.

I know that sometimes, I let my emotions get the best of me. When we argue, or when I see you leaving to hang out with someone else, I get scared, and I let my anger show in ways I wish it wouldn't. but that's something i'm working on. I never want to push you away because of my

WE AIN'T KIDS ANYMORE 25

own fears. Please know that it's not about you, it's about me trying to understand how to handle these feelings.

But even when I fall short, you never stop being the person I admire the most. I love your bright smile—it lights up every room you're in, and your tallness makes me feel small in the best way. I laugh at your corny jokes because they're a reflection of your heart, always lighthearted, always caring, always ready to make others smile. I see how much you love helping people, and it inspires me to do the same, to be more like you.

I want you to know how much I cherish our future together. I imagine us in that big city, working hard at our high-paying jobs, creating the life we've always dreamed of, and giving our future kids a life full of love, opportunities, and everything we never had. It's a beautiful thought, and I believe in it. I believe in us.

Thank you for being the person I turn to in the best and worst of times. for all the things you do that show me you care, for loving me in ways that make me feel seen and valued. I love you more than words can express, and I can't wait to keep building our dreams together.

forever yours,

ce'azia

Life hurts
Especially when i can't be with you
All the time
1hr and 32 minutes can do alot to you
My guy pretty like a girl
Swimming laps through the pool water
Overheated like i'm underworld
Sometimes i get scared
Because it feels like you don't care
Enlighten me on what i can do to be better
Because i feel like i try to hard an i fail
And i can't shake the feeling of losing you

Again , because once you're tied to a person
Its like untying a double knot in a pair of jordans
My heart could never let go. God bless my heart if i ever
Have to go through heartbreak. And not just
With boys or girls . in general . we're so tied to each other
When one of us tries to leave the universe brings us back to
Each other. And some days i'll sit and talk to the moon
About all the things we could be or will be. And the moon talks back
To tell me not to worry that you will have what you envisioned
But I love talking to the sun because she sees all the good in you like I do.
She'll tell you that we are still young trying to figure everything out. And
that we still have time. And that true lovers will never be separated for
long. The stars will tell you that you shine just as bright as they do . that
you have so much potential. And that's why i love talking to them about
you

I'd trade my whole life just to be one of those girls

i wonder if you feel it too
the way my heart skips a beat
every time you look at me,
like time pauses, just for a second.
it's like we're made of stars,
burning bright in the middle of the night,
but somehow, no one can see us
except for the moon.
we've got this thing that's hard to explain,
like an electric current that runs through my veins
whenever you're near,
and I just want to hold on to it forever.
your voice is like a song i can't get out of my head,
the kind that sticks with you,
even after the music fades.
when you laugh, it's like my whole world lights up,
and I forget about the dark.
sometimes i get scared,
because i don't know if this is real,
but then i look at you,
and i remember what it feels like
to be alive, to be here,
to be with you.
we're not perfect,

but that's what makes us feel so right.
it's like we're both trying to figure it out
in our own broken way,
but somehow it all fits.
when you hold my hand,
everything feels so easy,
like all the weight of the world
just disappears for a little while.
and i don't need anything more
than the way your fingers feel
intertwined with mine.
sometimes i lie awake at night
thinking about the future,
about the life we could have,
but then i realize
that right now, this moment,
is all I need.
there are days when i feel lost,
but your smile brings me back,
like a lighthouse guiding me home,
and suddenly, i remember
how much you mean to me.
i hope you see me the way i see you—
not just in the good moments,
but in all of it,
the messy, imperfect parts,
because I wouldn't want to share this with anyone else.

---

there are days when my mind is loud,
and the silence between us feels heavy,
but then you say something small,
and suddenly the noise disappears.

WE AIN'T KIDS ANYMORE

it's like your words are the only thing that matter,
the only thing that makes sense.
i think about us sometimes,
and i wonder how we got here,
how we found each other in a world so big,
and yet it feels like we were always meant to be.
like this was the plan all along,
even if we didn't know it yet.
i love how you can make me feel safe
even when the world outside is falling apart.
your presence is my anchor,
your love is the water that keeps me afloat,
and i wonder if you even realize
how much you mean to me.
sometimes i get scared,
scared of losing you,
scared of this love slipping through my fingers
like sand, like everything else does.
but then you pull me close,
and everything feels like it's going to be okay.
i know i'm not always easy to love,
but i hope you see past my walls,
see the soft parts i keep hidden away
because I trust you with them.
you've shown me that i don't have to be perfect,
i don't have to have all the answers,
i just have to be me,
and that's enough for you.
some days, i wish i could freeze time,
so i could stay in these moments forever,
with you beside me,
laughing at nothing,

talking about everything,
sharing our dreams like they're real,
like they're already happening.
i want to be with you in every season,
through every change.
i want to hold your hand in the summer,
when everything feels endless and warm,
and in the winter,
when the cold wind blows,
but your love keeps me close.
there are times when i wonder if you really know
how much i need you,
how much i want you,
how much i love you.
because when you're around,
everything feels right,
and when you're not,
It's like there's a piece of me missing.
but i'm learning that love isn't just about the good days,
it's about the bad ones too,
the days when we argue,
when we don't understand each other,
but still, we try.
because that's what love is—
it's not perfect,
it's not always easy,
but it's always worth it.
i don't need you to save me,
i don't need you to fix me,
but i need you to be here,
to hold me when i'm falling apart,
to laugh with me when things are light,

WE AIN'T KIDS ANYMORE

to remind me of who i am
when I forget.
and even though i don't always say it,
even though sometimes my fears get in the way,
i'm so grateful for you,
for everything you do,
for every little thing that makes me feel seen,
like the way you send me songs
that make me feel like you're speaking to me,
or how you always know when something's wrong
even when I try to hide it.
you're the calm in my chaos,
the warmth in my coldest moments,
the light in the darkness
That makes me feel like I'm not alone.
and i hope you know that i see you,
every part of you,
the good, the bad, the messy,
and I love you for all of it.
some days i wonder what the future holds,
but then i think about all the things we'll do,
the places we'll go,
the life we'll build.
because I believe in us.
I believe in what we're becoming.
and i know that whatever happens,
we'll make it through,
because we're stronger together.
so here's my heart,
laid bare and unguarded,
because I trust you with it.
i trust you to hold it close,

to protect it,
to love it like you love me.
and i know there will be times
when it's hard,
when we feel lost or unsure,
but i'm willing to walk through all of that with you,
because you're the one i want by my side,
through every high, every low,
every little moment in between.
and when the world feels too big
and everything seems out of control,
i'll look at you,
and i'll remember that love is all we need,
because with you, i've already found everything
i ever wanted to.
i try not to care,
but it's hard when everything reminds me of you,
when every song i listen to feels like it's written for us.
sometimes i wanna act like i'm fine,
like nothing bothers me,
like i'm invincible,
but the truth is,
i miss you when you're not around,
i think about you when i'm supposed to be doing something else,
and i can't shake the feeling
that maybe i'm falling too hard.
but i guess that's what happens
when you let someone in
and they start becoming a part of your world,
when you start caring
even though you said you wouldn't.
sometimes i tell myself i don't need you,

WE AIN'T KIDS ANYMORE

i try to act tough,
like i'm better off without you,
but deep down,
I know that's not true.
because without you,
Everything feels a little emptier.
i could pretend i don't care,
but we both know that's a lie.
i could act like i'm fine,
but I'm not.
and i don't know if you even see it,
the way i look at you like you're the only thing that matters.
i know i shouldn't care this much,
but I do.
and it scares me,
because the more i care,
the harder it is to let go.
and that's the thing
I don't want to let go.
i think about the way we talk,
how it feels like we can say anything,
and i know i get scared sometimes,
but you always bring me back,
you always remind me that it's okay to feel,
it's okay to be a little messy,
to not have everything figured out.
sometimes i want to shut everything out,
become numb to it all,
just like Lil Peep says,
"i don't give a f*ck,"
but I know that's not really who I am.
because i do care,

even when I try to pretend I don't.
i'm trying to find balance,
trying to figure out how to love without losing myself.
but maybe that's the thing,
maybe i'm supposed to lose myself a little
when I love someone like you.
maybe it's okay to fall,
to get caught up in this mess of emotions,
to let myself feel something real
for the first time in a long while.
i don't want to keep pretending,
pretending i'm fine when i'm not,
pretending I'm strong when I'm not.
because i need you to see me,
to see the parts of me that are afraid,
the parts that are unsure,
the parts that just want to be loved.
maybe we're both figuring it out,
trying to make sense of everything,
but i'm not giving up on us,
even when things get complicated,
even when we fight,
even when we don't know what's next.
because the truth is,
I need you in ways I can't explain.
and when i'm with you,
i feel like i'm home,
like all the chaos inside me
stops for a second.
maybe i don't need to have it all figured out,
maybe it's enough to just be with you,
to ride out the highs and lows,

and just let life happen as it comes.
and if i'm honest,
i don't care what anyone says,
this love, this mess,
it's ours.
it's ours to figure out,
ours to hold on to,
ours to break and heal and build again.
so even when the world feels heavy,
when things don't make sense,
i'll keep holding on to you,
because deep down,
i know that you're the one
i want to keep close,
the one i want to keep loving.
you're the one i can't shake,
the one who's always on my mind.
and maybe i don't always say it,
but i hope you know that i care more than i let on,
more than I'm willing to admit.
and i'll keep telling myself
that it's okay to care,
that it's okay to want you,
because sometimes,
That's all I really need.

---

there are nights when i feel like i'm falling apart
but i don't want to admit it.
i try to pretend like i've got it all together,
but deep down, i'm just holding on
to the pieces of myself that still make sense.
you know that feeling, don't you?

like everything is slipping through your fingers
but you keep pretending like you're fine.
sometimes i wish i could show you
what's going on inside my head,
the way my thoughts get tangled up
when i think about us,
the way my heart beats faster
whenever you smile at me.
but instead, i just hide it,
because it feels too messy,
too real,
too much for anyone to understand.
but you do understand, don't you?
you see me when i'm not looking,
you see the cracks in my smile
and the way i try to cover up the tears
when i think no one's watching.
you know all the things i'm too scared to say,
all the things i hide behind my walls,
but you don't walk away.
you stay,
and that means more than words can explain.
i know i'm not perfect,
i know i've got my flaws,
but when i'm with you,
it feels like none of that matters.
you love me in ways i never thought possible,
you see past the broken pieces,
and you love me anyway.
sometimes i wonder if you ever get tired of me,
of my mood swings,
of the way i can't always express myself,

WE AIN'T KIDS ANYMORE

of the way i get caught up in my head
and push you away without meaning to.
but then you hold me,
and all those doubts disappear,
because i know you're not going anywhere.
you remind me that we're still learning,
still growing,
still figuring this all out.
we're not supposed to have all the answers,
and maybe that's the beauty of it.
we get to take our time,
make mistakes,
and find our way back to each other.
sometimes i get mad at myself for caring so much,
but i can't help it.
i care because you matter to me,
because every moment we share is important,
and i never want to take it for granted.
even when i act like i don't need you,
deep down, i'm just scared of getting hurt,
scared of letting someone in and losing them.
but then you remind me that it's okay to love,
that it's okay to let go of control,
that it's okay to be vulnerable.
and in those moments,
i realize that maybe i don't need to have all the walls up.
maybe it's okay to just be myself,
with all my imperfections,
and let you love me anyway.
i think about the future sometimes,
about what it will look like when we're not just
trying to figure things out,

but building a life we're proud of.
i imagine us walking through the city,
hand in hand,
with nothing to stop us.
i picture us in our own little world,
making memories,
sharing secrets,
laughing at nothing,
because we'll have everything we need
right there with each other.
i know it's not going to be easy,
there will be days when we feel lost,
days when we question everything,
but i also know that we'll always find our way back.
because we're tied to each other,
and no matter how far we wander,
we'll always find a way back home.
so even when i act like i don't care,
when i try to hide behind my pride,
know that you're the only one i want,
the only one i need.
because you've become a part of me,
and there's no way i'm letting go.
i'll keep telling myself it's okay to feel,
that it's okay to want you,
that it's okay to let myself love you
without holding back.
because with you,
it feels like i've found something real.
something worth fighting for.
and maybe we're not perfect,
maybe we're both still figuring this out,

WE AIN'T KIDS ANYMORE

but that's what makes us us,
and I wouldn't change a thing.
because when i'm with you,
everything feels right,
even in the mess,
even in the chaos.
It feels like home.
sometimes i find myself drifting back,
to the way we used to talk about everything,
and nothing,
all at once.
i miss the way your voice would break the silence,
like the first light of dawn,
soft, quiet,
but somehow so real.
i think about those nights,
how we didn't need words to say what we meant,
how everything felt easy,
how everything just... made sense.
but time changes things, doesn't it?
we both grew up,
but i don't know if we grew together.
maybe we did,
but sometimes it feels like we've become strangers,
still tied to each other,
but in ways i can't quite explain.
it's like we're stuck between the past and the present,
wondering where we fit in this future we keep talking about.
there are days when i can feel you next to me,
like we never left,
like we're still that version of us
that was unbreakable,

that was fearless,
that was invincible.
but then i blink,
and it's gone,
and i realize we can't go back,
we can't rewrite what's already been written.
i think about how things used to be,
and part of me wishes i could hold on to that forever,
but i can't.
i know we both have our own paths now,
but there's still this part of me that holds on,
just a little too tightly,
because letting go feels impossible,
like giving up on something that was once everything.
but maybe that's the way love is,
you know?
it stays with you,
even when you try to forget it,
even when you try to bury it deep,
it lingers,
in the corners of your heart,
in the corners of your mind.
and every now and then,
you catch a glimpse of it,
like a fleeting memory,
like the way the sun hits the water
just before it sets.
and that's the part that gets to me,
the part where you're still there,
even though we're not.
because love doesn't just disappear.
it stays,

in the cracks of who we are,
in the places we didn't think to look.
it stays in the moments we didn't realize mattered
until they were gone.
but maybe it's better this way,
maybe it's better to keep the memories,
to hold on to the love we shared
without trying to force something that's not there anymore.
maybe it's okay to let go of the idea of us,
while still holding on to the parts of you
that made me believe in everything.
sometimes i wonder what you think about,
if you ever look back,
if you ever think about the things we used to say,
about the things we used to dream about.
i wonder if you still see me the way i see you,
if you still feel that spark,
that fire,
or if it's just gone,
faded into the past like everything else.
and maybe that's the hardest part,
wondering if you still think of me,
if you still care,
even in the quiet moments,
even in the moments when we're not together,
when the world feels so big,
and i feel so small,
and i wonder if i've lost you for good.
but i keep telling myself that it's okay,
that everything happens for a reason,
that we're both just trying to find our way,
even if it means walking different paths.

i remind myself that love isn't about holding on forever,
it's about the moments we shared,
the times we were close,
the feelings we had,
even if they were only for a while.
and sometimes,
when i lie awake at night,
i talk to the stars,
like they're my old friends,
asking them questions i don't have answers to,
wondering if they know what it's like
to love someone and let them go.
and they just shine back at me,
like they understand,
like they've been through it too.
maybe that's what it means to grow,
to love without knowing the end,
to let go without forgetting,
to move forward while carrying the past with you.
maybe that's how we learn,
by falling and getting back up,
by trying and failing and trying again.
maybe that's what we're supposed to do,
to keep learning how to love,
even when it doesn't look the way we thought it would.
but you'll always be a part of me,
even when i can't see you,
even when we're not together.
and i think that's what matters.
that no matter where life takes us,
no matter how far apart we get,
we'll always have that moment,

that spark,
that fire,
that once made everything feel like it was ours.
and i'll carry that with me,
forever,
because that's the kind of love
that never really goes away.
i think about the times we talked about forever,
like it was something that could never slip through our fingers,
like it was a promise we made without even saying it.
but forever isn't as easy as we thought,
and i guess that's the thing,
life doesn't always follow the script we make.
it doesn't always go the way we plan.
and sometimes,
we're left with the memories,
the words we said,
the love we felt,
wondering if it was enough.
i remember the way your hand felt in mine,
the way everything seemed right in those moments,
how we talked about the future,
about what we could be,
like we were already living in it,
like it was already ours.
but then, slowly,
it started slipping away,
and i wasn't sure if i was holding on too tightly,
or if you were letting go.
i used to think love was something you could hold forever,
something you could keep,
like a piece of yourself that no one could take away.

but i've learned that love is fleeting,
it comes and goes like the tide,
like the seasons changing,
and sometimes,
it's okay to let it pass.
because maybe that's how we grow,
by letting things go,
even when it feels impossible,
even when every part of us is screaming not to.
but when i look back,
when i look at the pieces of us that are still there,
i realize that the love we had wasn't lost,
it's just transformed.
maybe it's not the same as it was,
but it's still here,
in the way i remember you,
in the way i feel when i think about us.
and i don't think that will ever change,
no matter where life takes us.
sometimes i catch myself waiting for a sign,
waiting for something to tell me that it's okay,
waiting for the universe to make sense of all the mess.
but i've learned that the signs aren't always clear,
that sometimes, you have to create your own path,
you have to decide what comes next.
and maybe that's what i'm still learning,
how to let go of the things i can't control,
how to trust that things will fall into place,
even if it takes time.
you know, i've spent so much time
worrying about what's gone,
about what we could've been,

WE AIN'T KIDS ANYMORE

but now,
i try to focus on what we had,
on the moments we shared,
because those are the things that will stay with me.
those are the things that remind me
that love, even if it doesn't last forever,
is still worth everything.
so here i am,
learning to let go,
learning to trust in the flow of life,
learning that love isn't always about holding on,
but sometimes, it's about letting go,
about accepting the things that are out of our hands,
and finding peace in the moments we had,
the love we shared,
and knowing that it was enough.
i don't need forever to know that we were real,
i don't need to hold on to everything
to understand that you changed me,
that you taught me how to love,
how to feel,
how to be vulnerable.
and even though things aren't the same,
i'll always carry that with me.
sometimes, i wonder if you're thinking of me,
if you remember the little things,
like the way we laughed until we couldn't breathe,
or the way we'd talk about our dreams
like they were already true,
like we could make anything happen.
and i hope you do,
because i still think about those moments,

even when it feels like they're just memories now.
i guess that's the thing with love,
it doesn't always stay the same,
but it doesn't have to.
it can be something beautiful even in its change,
even in its imperfection.
because when it's real,
it stays with you,
no matter how much time passes,
no matter how much distance there is.
and i'll keep holding on to that,
the love we had,
the way we made each other better,
even when we didn't know it.
because that's the kind of love
that stays with you forever,
even when it fades into something else.
and maybe that's what i've been afraid of all along,
that one day,
i wouldn't have you anymore,
that i wouldn't be able to find you in the memories,
in the spaces we once shared.
but now, i see it differently,
i see that we'll always have the love we shared,
even if it's not what we thought it would be.
we'll always have that piece of us
that will never go away.
so i'll stop waiting for a sign,
i'll stop looking for something to fix what's broken,
and i'll start living in the moments we had,
in the love we shared,
because that's enough.

WE AIN'T KIDS ANYMORE

and it always will be.
sometimes i think about the times we sat in silence,
just being in each other's presence,
not needing anything but the quiet comfort of knowing
we were right there, together.
those moments felt so full,
so complete,
like we didn't need words to speak to each other.
and maybe that's what i miss the most,
the ease of being with you,
the way everything felt effortless
when we didn't try too hard.
but now it feels like every word is weighed down,
like every conversation has to mean something,
like we've forgotten how to just be,
how to just exist in the same space without overthinking it.
maybe we've changed,
maybe we've grown in different directions,
but i still wonder if we'll ever find that place again,
where we don't need to talk to understand,
where silence feels like home instead of a void.
it's strange, isn't it?
how time does that to people,
how it stretches out moments
and makes you look at things from a different angle.
we used to be so sure,
so certain of everything we wanted,
everything we believed in.
but now, it's like we're constantly searching
for something we can't quite name,
for something we've already lost,
but don't know how to get back.

and maybe that's okay.
maybe it's okay to not have all the answers,
to not know what comes next.
because sometimes,
the journey is the answer.
maybe we weren't meant to stay the same,
maybe we were always supposed to change,
to grow into different versions of ourselves.
and in doing so,
we learn more about who we are
and who we want to be.
and i guess that's the thing,
isn't it?
you can't hold on to something forever,
no matter how much you want to.
love, it shifts, it bends,
it becomes something else,
and that's part of the beauty of it.
it's not about holding tight,
but about letting go,
about trusting that the love you had
will evolve into something else,
something just as beautiful,
just as real,
but different.
so i let myself feel what i feel,
even when it's messy,
even when it doesn't make sense.
i let myself feel the ache,
the longing,
because i know it's just part of the process.
i know that i'm learning,

WE AIN'T KIDS ANYMORE

that we're learning,
and that's all we can do—
keep moving forward,
keep figuring it out as we go.
but i can't help but think about the future sometimes,
about the way we used to talk about it,
like we had it all figured out.
but we didn't, did we?
none of us do.
we were just kids,
dreaming big,
thinking we could conquer everything.
and maybe we still can.
maybe we'll get there,
even if it takes longer than we thought.
maybe we'll find our way back,
even if it's not the same path we were once on.
so maybe i'll stop searching for answers
and start trusting the questions,
trusting that everything will fall into place
in its own time.
maybe i'll stop looking back,
and start looking forward,
not to find the person i used to be,
but to discover the person i'm becoming.
and maybe, just maybe,
when we're ready,
we'll find each other again.
in a new place,
in a new time,
when we're different,
but still the same.

and we'll remember the love we had,
and know that it was always enough,
even if it didn't last forever.
so until then,
i'll carry the memories with me,
i'll carry the love with me,
and i'll keep moving forward,
trusting that everything happens for a reason.
and when i look at the stars at night,
i'll think of you,
and i'll remember that we were once
everything to each other.
and i'll be grateful for that,
because even if it's over,
it was real,
and that's all that matters.
sometimes, when i close my eyes,
i can still hear the way you said my name,
like it was something only you could say,
like it held more meaning than just letters.
and i wonder if you still say it the same way,
if it still feels the same when you say it,
or if it's just another word in a world full of noise.
and i can't help but wish that we could go back
to those moments when everything was simple,
when we were both just trying to figure out
what we wanted,
but we had all the time in the world
to figure it out together.
but time doesn't wait,
it doesn't pause for us to catch up,
and sometimes, we fall behind

WE AIN'T KIDS ANYMORE

without realizing how far we've drifted.
it's not anyone's fault,
it's just the way life is,
and sometimes,
we just have to accept that.
and i think that's the hardest part—
accepting that things change,
that people change,
and that we don't always get to control it.
sometimes, love isn't enough to keep two people together,
even if you want it more than anything.
sometimes, you just have to let go,
and hope that the love you shared
will stay with you,
in the quiet moments,
in the small things that remind you of each other.
i used to think that love meant forever,
that if you loved someone enough,
nothing could tear you apart.
but love is more complicated than that.
love is about timing,
it's about being at the right place in your life
when the other person is too.
and sometimes,
you're just not in the same place,
even if you're both trying so hard
to make it work.
so i've learned to be okay with it,
to be okay with not having all the answers,
to be okay with the space between us.
because sometimes, distance is the only thing that can make you realize
how much you've grown,

how much you've changed.
and sometimes,
you have to let yourself grow alone
before you can grow together again.
but i still think about you,
about the way we used to laugh,
about the way you used to look at me
like i was everything.
and maybe that's the thing i'll never let go of,
the way you made me feel,
the way you made me believe
that love could be simple,
that it could be easy,
that it could be ours.
but life isn't always simple,
and love isn't always easy.
sometimes, it's messy,
it's complicated,
and it's hard to see the end.
but maybe that's okay,
maybe that's the way it's supposed to be.
maybe we're supposed to learn from the hard parts,
to find our way back to each other,
even if it takes time.
and if we don't,
if we never find our way back,
I'll still carry the love we shared with me,
because that's something no one can take away.
it's something that will stay with me,
even in the quiet moments,
even in the times when I'm not sure where I'm going,
even when I'm not sure if I'll ever find someone like you again.

WE AIN'T KIDS ANYMORE

and maybe that's the beauty of love—
it doesn't need to last forever to be real.
it doesn't need to stay the same to be meaningful.
it just needs to be felt,
just needs to exist,
and leave a mark on your heart
that stays long after it's gone.
so when I look back,
I'll remember you,
I'll remember us,
and I'll be grateful for everything we had.
because even if it didn't last,
even if we changed,
even if we grew apart,
we were once everything to each other.
and that's enough.
and when the stars come out at night,
I'll look up,
and I'll think of you,
because even though we've both moved on,
even though we've both changed,
you'll always be a part of me,
in the quiet moments,
in the spaces between us,
in the way love still lingers,
even when it's not the same.
Continuing the exploration of love, change, and moving forward:
---
some days, i wake up and feel like i'm still holding on
to pieces of you,
like i'm carrying the weight of everything we were,
trying to make sense of it all.
but the truth is,

sometimes i wonder if i'm just holding on to the past,
wondering if you still think of me
the way i think of you.
but i can't keep living in that space,
can't keep waiting for something to change,
for the door to open and bring us back together
like we never left.
maybe that's the hardest part of growing up,
letting go of things you can't control,
things you can't fix.
i've spent so many days wishing we could have done things differently,
wishing i could turn back time and fix the mistakes
that led us here.
but i've learned that time doesn't work that way,
it doesn't go backwards,
it only moves forward.
and all i can do is keep moving,
keep living,
keep learning from everything that came before.
sometimes, i catch myself missing you
in the smallest, quietest ways,
like when i hear a song that used to be ours,
or when i see something that reminds me of you.
and it's funny how those moments still take me by surprise,
how a simple thing can bring everything rushing back.
but i think i've learned to accept that those moments are just part of the process,
part of growing,
part of healing.
and maybe it's okay to miss you,
maybe it's okay to still feel the pull of what we had,
because that's just another part of loving.

but i know now that i can't keep waiting for the past to come back.
i can't keep living in the memories,
wishing for things that will never be.
because the truth is,
we're both changing,
we're both moving forward,
and maybe that's where we're meant to be.
maybe this is how we grow,
by letting go of the things we can't change,
and trusting that the future will bring what's meant for us.
sometimes, when i look ahead,
i wonder if you're out there,
living your life,
finding new experiences,
new people,
new love.
and a part of me is happy for you,
happy that you're finding your way,
even if it's not with me.
because you deserve to be happy,
to find the things that make you feel whole,
just like i deserve to do the same.
i used to think that love meant finding your person,
holding on to them forever,
never letting go.
but now i see that love isn't about possession,
it's about freedom.
it's about allowing each other to be who you are,
to grow and change and evolve,
even if that means you're not always together.
because sometimes, love is letting go
so that you both can become who you were meant to be.

i'm learning that now,
learning that love doesn't always look the way we think it should,
and sometimes, the love you have for someone
isn't meant to last forever,
but it still leaves an imprint,
a mark that doesn't fade.
and maybe that's the real beauty of love,
the way it changes you,
even when it's no longer what you thought it would be.
and even though it hurts sometimes,
even though i still miss you in ways i can't explain,
i know it's okay to let go.
it's okay to let the past rest where it belongs
and look forward to what comes next.
because even though we don't have each other in the way we once did,
we'll always be a part of each other's story,
a chapter in a book that we'll never forget,
no matter where life takes us.
so here i am,
letting go,
letting the love we shared transform into something new,
something that's just as beautiful,
even if it's not what i expected.
and i'm okay with that.
i'm okay with the change,
with the growth,
with the journey ahead.
because i know that love, in its truest form,
will always be enough,
no matter how it looks,
no matter how it feels.
and i can't help but smile when i think of us,

WE AIN'T KIDS ANYMORE

those moments when everything felt light,
like we were floating on a cloud of happiness
that we never wanted to come down from.
i remember the times we laughed so hard
that we forgot what we were laughing about,
just the sound of joy echoing between us
like the sweetest song.
those are the moments that still make me feel full,
still make me feel warm,
like the sun is shining just a little bit brighter
when i think of you.
there was something so simple,
so pure,
about the way we connected,
like everything else in the world
faded away when we were together.
it wasn't about the big gestures,
it was about the small things,
the way we'd hold hands while we walked,
the way we'd make each other playlists,
the way we'd talk about the future
like we had all the time in the world
to make it happen.
and i still think about those dreams,
those plans we talked about
in the quiet moments,
like when we'd sit on the hood of your car
and look up at the stars,
talking about everything and nothing at all,
just being with each other.
it felt like we were the only two people in the world,
like we had our own little universe

where everything made sense.
it was beautiful, wasn't it?
how we could just be,
how we could make the ordinary feel special,
how we could take the smallest moments
and turn them into memories that would last forever.
and maybe that's the thing i'll always carry with me,
the way you made me feel
like i was enough,
like every part of me,
every little piece,
was something worth loving.
and even though things have changed,
even though we've gone our separate ways,
there's still a part of me that feels light,
that feels like i'm holding on to all the good,
to all the moments that still make me smile.
i think that's what love is,
not just the grand gestures or the promises,
but the quiet moments,
the laughter,
the memories that come rushing back
when you least expect it.
i'm grateful for all of it,
for every second we spent together,
for every late-night conversation,
for every inside joke that will always make me laugh.
and i'm happy, too,
because even though we've both moved on,
i know we both found something special in each other,
something real,
something that was always meant to be,

even if it didn't last forever.
because love isn't about forever,
it's about the now,
about the way it makes you feel in the moment,
about the way it changes you,
even if it's just for a little while.
and i'll carry that with me,
that feeling of being loved,
of being seen,
of being happy in someone's presence
without needing anything else.
so i'm okay,
i'm happy,
because i know that we were always meant to meet,
always meant to share those moments.
and maybe we'll cross paths again one day,
maybe we won't,
but no matter what,
i'll always look back with a smile,
grateful for the love we shared,
for the laughter we gave,
for the memories we made.
and every time i look up at the sky,
i'll think of you,
and i'll smile,
because i know that love isn't about holding on,
it's about appreciating what was,
and being thankful for the happiness
it brought into our lives.
and maybe, just maybe,
that's enough.
there's something so peaceful about knowing

that love doesn't always have to be complicated,
that sometimes, it's just two people
sharing little moments of happiness,
and feeling the world slow down around them.
i think that's what i'll always remember the most,
those quiet mornings when we'd wake up,
all tangled in the sheets,
smiling like we had no care in the world.
just being together,
and knowing that was all we needed.
there's a certain magic in simplicity,
in the way we could laugh over the smallest things,
in the way you made me feel like i was home,
no matter where we were.
those moments when time didn't matter,
when the world felt still,
like we were the only two people who existed,
and nothing else could compare to that feeling.
it was so easy to fall into that rhythm,
to let go of everything else and just be.
we didn't need anything extravagant,
no grand gestures or fancy dates,
just each other.
and somehow, that made everything more beautiful,
more real.
and even though things have changed,
i still carry that feeling with me,
like a little piece of sunshine in my heart.
there are days when i miss those simple moments,
when i catch myself smiling at the thought of you,
thinking about how easy it was to be with you.
and it makes me believe that maybe love isn't about forever,

WE AIN'T KIDS ANYMORE

it's about finding the right person at the right time,
and making the most of every second.
and even if it doesn't last forever,
it was still beautiful,
still worth every moment.
i think the thing i'll always appreciate
is the way you made me feel like i could be myself,
without fear, without hesitation.
you never asked me to change,
you never tried to mold me into someone i wasn't.
you just accepted me,
in all my messiness,
in all my imperfections,
and that's something i'll never forget.
sometimes, i'll think back on those late nights,
those quiet conversations,
and i'll remember the way your voice sounded
when you told me everything would be okay.
and maybe we were just two kids trying to figure it out,
but in those moments,
it felt like we had everything we needed.
and i'm okay with that now,
i'm okay with the way things turned out.
because i know that love is always going to look different,
and that's what makes it so special.
we don't need to have everything figured out,
we don't need to have all the answers,
we just need to be present,
to feel the love that's right in front of us.
so here i am,
smiling because i know that even though we've changed,
we've grown,

we've moved on,
we still carry a piece of each other.
and maybe that's all that matters.
the love we shared,
the memories we made,
and the way we made each other feel,
like we were enough,
just as we were.
and when i look back,
i'll think of you with a smile,
because you taught me that love doesn't need to be perfect,
it just needs to be real.
and that's enough.
that's more than enough.
and maybe that's the secret to it all,
to love with everything you have,
even when you know that time is fleeting,
even when you know that things won't always stay the same.
because love, when it's pure,
it doesn't ask for forever,
it just asks to be felt in the moment.
to be shared,
to be lived.
and in those moments,
i remember how easy it was to love you,
how natural it felt to be close,
to share the smallest pieces of our days
and turn them into something extraordinary.
it's funny how love can do that—
take the simplest things,
the quiet moments,
and turn them into memories

that stay with you long after they've passed.
like the time we stayed up all night talking about everything
and nothing at all.
i remember the way the stars seemed to shimmer just for us,
like they were listening,
like they knew our dreams,
knew our hearts.
and in those moments,
i felt so connected to you,
like our souls were dancing in sync,
moving with the rhythm of the universe.
it wasn't perfect,
and maybe it wasn't meant to last forever,
but it was beautiful.
beautiful in the way we loved without hesitation,
without fear,
just two people trying to figure it all out together.
and that's something i'll always hold close,
the way we made everything feel so right,
even when the world around us was uncertain.
it's funny how life works,
how we can meet someone and feel like
you've known them forever,
like they were always meant to be a part of your story.
and even when the story changes,
even when the chapters shift and turn,
the love we shared stays with us.
like a soft light that never really fades,
but continues to glow softly in the background.
and i'm grateful for that,
for everything we were,
for everything we shared.

because even though we've moved on,
i know that those moments were real,
and they'll always be a part of me.
and i wouldn't change a thing,
because all of it,
the laughter, the late nights,
the small moments,
they made me who i am today.
and so now,
i look ahead,
with hope and excitement
for everything that's to come.
because life is still unfolding,
and love is still waiting,
in all the new adventures,
in the new people we'll meet,
in the new stories we'll create.
but i carry the lessons from you with me,
carry the love that we shared,
because it's shaped me,
and it's made me ready for whatever's next.
and maybe that's the beauty of love—
it doesn't stay the same,
but it leaves something behind,
something lasting,
something worth remembering.
and so i'll keep moving forward,
with a heart full of gratitude,
and a mind full of dreams.
because love is always worth it,
even when it's just for a season,
even when it's not forever.

WE AIN'T KIDS ANYMORE

because every moment is enough,
every laugh, every tear,
every quiet conversation under the stars,
it's all part of the story,
and i'm thankful for every chapter we shared.
and who knows?
maybe one day,
we'll look back and smile at how far we've come,
at how much we've grown.
but for now,
i'm just happy to be here,
happy to have loved,
happy to have experienced something so beautiful,
even if it wasn't forever.
because the memories,
the love,
the joy we shared—
that's what lasts.
and that's enough.
and sometimes, when the world feels too loud,
too fast,
i think back to those moments with you,
to the quiet ones,
the ones that felt like they could last forever.
those are the memories i hold close now,
the ones that remind me that not all love is meant to stay,
but every love teaches us something.
and i learned so much from you,
from the way you loved me,
from the way you made me feel seen,
like i was exactly where i was meant to be.
and maybe that's the real magic of it all—

the way love, no matter how fleeting,
creates something in us that can't be erased.
you showed me what it means to give all of yourself,
to share your heart,
to love without holding back.
and even though we've both moved on,
i know that part of you will always be with me,
in the way i see the world,
in the way i love others.
i'll take that with me,
the lessons and the love,
and carry it into the next chapter of my life,
knowing that no matter what comes next,
i'm stronger because of what we had.
and that's a gift,
something i'll always be thankful for.
so when i look ahead,
i do it with hope,
with excitement for the future,
because i know that love is a constant evolution.
and i know that, even when things seem uncertain,
we're always growing,
always learning,
always becoming who we're meant to be.
and if the universe brings us together again,
or if our paths cross in some unexpected way,
i'll be ready.
ready to see what's next,
to embrace the person i've become,
the person you helped shape.
and if not,
i'll still carry the love we shared with me,

WE AIN'T KIDS ANYMORE 67

like a light that will never go out,
like a warmth that stays in my heart,
because no matter what,
i'm grateful for the time we had.
and so now, i walk forward,
feeling the breeze of new beginnings,
knowing that the past is behind me,
but it's not forgotten.
it's part of me,
it's part of the person i'm becoming.
and with every step i take,
i know i'm closer to the person i'm meant to be,
to the life i'm meant to live.
and i hope, wherever you are,
you're doing the same—
walking your path,
finding your peace,
and holding onto the love that's out there for you.
because i know you deserve it,
just as much as i do.
and we'll both be okay.
we'll both find our way.
and when the sun rises again,
i'll think of you with a smile,
because i know that everything that happened,
all the love,
all the moments,
all the lessons,
were meant to be.
and that's enough.
that's all i need.
and there are days when i'll still feel the weight of it all,

when the memories hit me like a wave,
and i'll wonder what could have been.
but even in those moments,
i won't regret it.
because everything we shared was real,
and nothing can take that away.
not time,
not distance,
not change.
those moments will always be a part of me,
and i'll carry them with grace,
like a quiet strength that reminds me of my own resilience.
i've learned that love isn't always about forever,
it's about the moments that change you,
the people who leave an imprint on your soul,
no matter how long they stay.
and i'll always be grateful for the way you made me feel seen,
for the way you cared for me when i didn't always know how to care for myself.
you taught me the beauty of being vulnerable,
of letting go and trusting in something real.
and while we may never be together again,
i know that i'll look back on our time
with a heart full of gratitude,
because it was a love that helped me grow,
a love that shaped me into someone stronger,
someone wiser.
and i know that's what matters.
because love is never wasted,
it's always an opportunity to learn,
to evolve,
to become the person you're meant to be.

so now, as i stand here looking ahead,
i feel a sense of peace.
i'm not afraid of what comes next,
because i know that i am enough.
i know that love will come again,
and when it does,
i'll be ready.
i'll be open,
and i'll embrace it fully,
just as i did with you.
because no matter where we go,
no matter where life leads us,
i know we'll both be okay.
we'll both find the happiness we deserve,
the love that feels like home.
and i'll keep you in my heart,
always,
not as a reminder of what was lost,
but as a symbol of what was found.
and when the world feels heavy,
when things get tough,
i'll look back on all we shared,
and i'll find the strength to keep going.
because love, real love,
never really leaves you.
it stays,
in the smallest ways,
in the quiet moments,
in the way you smile when you think of someone,
in the way you still feel their presence,
even when they're not there.
so here's to love,

in all its forms,
to the lessons it teaches,
to the hearts it touches.
here's to you,
to me,
to everything we were,
and everything we're becoming.
i'll carry you with me,
in the softest way,
like a memory that never fades,
like a part of me that will always be whole,
because of you.
and no matter where life takes us,
i'll always be thankful for the time we shared,
for the love we gave.
and so i'll walk forward,
with my head held high,
knowing that everything that happened,
all the love,
all the pain,
was part of something bigger,
something beautiful.
and now, i'm ready for whatever comes next.
i'm ready for the future,
for the love that's still waiting for me.
and i'll go into it,
knowing that i'll always have a piece of you with me,
and that's enough to keep me going.
and as the days go by,
i'll remember that love is never really lost.
it transforms,
it becomes a part of you,

and even though you may not see it in the same way anymore,
it still lingers in the background,
a soft reminder of all that once was.
and in those moments,
when i think of you,
i'll smile,
because i'll know that we gave each other something real.
something that was worth every bit of heartache,
worth every laugh,
every tear,
every second spent together.
and now, i walk with that love as a light,
guiding me through whatever comes next,
because i know that love doesn't disappear,
it just evolves,
it takes new forms,
and sometimes it's in the quietest of moments
that you'll feel it the most.
it's in the way the sun rises,
in the way the world keeps turning,
in the way people keep loving,
even when they don't have to.
and i'll keep loving,
too.
because love doesn't end just because someone walks out of your life.
it lives in the way you treat others,
in the way you care for the people you meet,
in the way you show up for the world around you.
and i'll keep showing up,
with an open heart,
ready for all that's ahead.
and i know that one day,

i'll look back and see how far i've come,
how much i've learned,
how much i've grown.
because everything i've been through,
all the joy and all the pain,
has made me stronger,
has made me ready for what comes next.
and i'll find love again,
maybe in unexpected places,
maybe in ways i didn't imagine.
but i'll welcome it,
because i know that love is always worth it,
even when it scares me,
even when it feels uncertain.
i'll be brave,
i'll be open,
because i know that love is what makes life beautiful.
and when that love comes,
i'll remember you,
and the lessons you taught me.
i'll remember how you made me feel,
how you helped me find pieces of myself i didn't know existed.
i'll remember the quiet moments,
the loud ones,
the messy ones,
the perfect ones.
and i'll carry that with me,
like a treasure,
like something too precious to forget.
because love is always worth it,
even when it feels impossible,
even when it feels like the world is too big,

too overwhelming.
because at the end of the day,
love is what makes us human,
it's what connects us all,
and no matter where we go,
we'll always find a way back to it.
so here's to the future,
to everything that's still ahead,
to all the love we've yet to give,
to all the dreams we've yet to chase.
because i'm not afraid anymore.
i'm not afraid of what's to come,
i'm not afraid of the unknown.
because i know that i'm strong enough to handle it,
strong enough to keep moving forward,
strong enough to love again.
and with that love,
i'll build something beautiful.
something lasting,
something real.
and i'll never forget the love we shared,
because it was a part of making me who i am.
and now, i'm ready for the rest of the story,
the rest of the journey,
and whatever that may look like,
i know it'll be something i'm proud of.
because i've learned that love is about more than just the ending,
it's about how you live it,
how you grow with it,
how you give it,
and how you let it shape you into the person you're meant to be.
and so, with that,

i say goodbye to the past,
thank you for everything we were,
thank you for everything we shared.
i carry it with me always,
and i move forward,
with my heart wide open,
ready for whatever comes next.
because love never really ends,
it just changes,
it evolves,
and i'm ready for the next chapter.
and as i walk through each new day,
i'll keep your lessons close,
the ones that taught me about love,
about patience,
about understanding.
i'll carry them in my bones,
in my heartbeat,
because they're a part of me now,
and no matter where i go,
they'll always be there,
guiding me,
reminding me of the strength
we both found in each other.
and maybe one day,
when the world feels quiet enough,
i'll hear your voice again in the back of my mind,
not with longing or regret,
but with gratitude.
i'll remember the warmth in your laugh,
the way you made me feel like i was enough,
even when i doubted myself.

WE AIN'T KIDS ANYMORE

and i'll smile,
because i'll know that the love we had,
however brief,
was more than enough.
the universe has a funny way of showing us what we need,
when we need it.
and i believe it brought us together for a reason,
even if that reason was just to show me how to love
and how to let go.
because sometimes,
the greatest act of love is knowing when to release,
when to let the winds of life take us where we need to go,
even if it's not where we expected.
but i'm not scared anymore.
i know that what's meant for me will find me,
just as you found me at the perfect time.
we both had lessons to learn,
we both had roads to walk,
and now, we're ready for new adventures,
new loves,
new chapters.
and i'll look back on us,
not with sadness,
but with the kind of smile that says,
"thank you for being part of my story."
because you were.
and i wouldn't change a thing.
so here's to whatever comes next.
i'm ready for it.
i'm ready to meet new faces,
to chase new dreams,
to discover new sides of myself.

but i'll never forget the version of me
that was shaped by us,
by you,
by everything we went through.
and when the day comes that i find new love,
i'll love it with all that i have,
knowing that it's built on a foundation of everything
i learned from loving you.
because you taught me that love isn't just about staying,
it's about becoming.
and i'm becoming someone stronger,
someone more open,
someone who knows that love is a journey,
not a destination.
so, thank you.
thank you for everything.
for the laughter,
for the late-night talks,
for the moments we shared.
you helped me grow,
and now i'll carry that growth with me,
into every new chapter,
into every new day.
and no matter where life takes me,
i'll always remember how love felt with you,
how it shaped me,
and how it'll continue to shape me,
forever.
as i step forward,
i do it with a quiet confidence,
a knowing that the future is unwritten,
but filled with endless possibilities.

WE AIN'T KIDS ANYMORE

the love we shared taught me that
there is beauty in uncertainty,
in letting go and trusting the process,
even when the road ahead isn't clear.
i'll keep walking,
one step at a time,
knowing that each moment
is an opportunity to grow,
to learn,
to love again.
and when the world feels heavy,
when life gets complicated,
i'll think of all the moments we shared,
the simple ones,
the ones that felt like home.
i'll remember the way your voice sounded
when you said my name,
the way we laughed over nothing at all,
the quiet moments that spoke louder than words.
and i'll take that with me,
like a shield against the days when things get tough,
a reminder that love, even in its most fleeting form,
leaves a lasting mark on your soul.
and i know that as time passes,
i'll change,
i'll grow,
but i'll always carry the lessons you taught me.
the way to love without fear,
the way to be vulnerable,
the way to give without expecting anything in return.
those lessons will guide me,
through the people i meet,

through the love i find,
through the challenges i face.
and when i look back,
i'll see all the steps i've taken,
and i'll smile,
because i know that every single one
led me to this moment,
led me to the person i am today.
and i'll be proud of who i've become,
because i'll know that i've been shaped by something real,
something beautiful.
and i'll keep that love inside me,
the love we shared,
as a part of my story,
because it's what has made me who i am.
and maybe, one day,
i'll tell someone else about it,
about the way it felt to be loved like that,
to give love like that.
and i'll do it with a sense of gratitude,
because i'll know that love,
in whatever form it comes,
is always worth it.
so as i keep walking forward,
i do it with hope.
hope that the future will be bright,
hope that i will find love again,
hope that i'll continue to grow into the person
i was always meant to be.
because love doesn't define us,
but it helps us find ourselves,
helps us understand what we're truly capable of,

helps us become the best version of who we are.
and when the time comes,
when love finds me again,
i'll be ready.
ready to give,
ready to receive,
ready to cherish every moment,
because now i know how precious those moments are.
and i'll look back,
not with longing,
but with a heart full of love
for the time we shared,
for the lessons learned,
and for the person i became because of you.
thank you for everything.
thank you for being part of my journey,
for helping me discover parts of myself
i didn't even know existed.
and no matter where life takes us,
no matter how much time passes,
i'll always carry a piece of you with me,
as a part of my story,
a part of my heart.
because love never truly ends,
it just transforms,
it becomes something new,
something that continues to shape us,
and i'm thankful for the way you've shaped me.
so i'll keep moving forward,
knowing that love,
true love,
will always find a way back to us.

and when it does,
i'll be ready to love again,
with all that i have,
all that i am,
because love is the most powerful thing we have.
it's what makes us human,
what connects us all.
and in that connection,
i find peace.
so here's to everything that's still ahead,
to all the love yet to come,
to the life we're still building,
one step at a time.
and i know that no matter what,
it will be beautiful,
because it's all part of the journey,
the journey of love,
and the journey of life.
and so, with a heart full of hope,
i step into the future,
ready for whatever comes next,
because i know that i am enough,
and i always will be.
and as i walk into the unknown,
i don't walk with fear,
i walk with anticipation,
with excitement for the things yet to come.
each day is a new opportunity,
a new chapter to be written,
and i know that i'll write it with a heart open wide,
ready for whatever life has in store.
because love, even in its absence,

WE AIN'T KIDS ANYMORE

still fills me up,
it still carries me forward,
and i'll never let go of that.
there's a freedom in knowing that everything changes,
and that's okay.
change isn't something to fear,
it's something to embrace,
because in change, there's growth,
there's evolution,
there's a chance to be better than before.
and i'm ready for that change.
i'm ready to be more,
to love more,
to experience life more fully.
and maybe, along the way,
i'll find pieces of you again,
not in the way i once knew,
but in new ways.
maybe i'll find your laughter in the way the wind blows,
or see your smile in the way the sun rises.
because love doesn't always leave when people do,
it lingers,
it stays with you in ways you don't always expect.
and i'll keep that love with me,
like a secret treasure,
a reminder of the beautiful things we shared,
the beautiful person you were to me.
but it's not just about holding onto the past,
it's about looking to the future,
about seeing what's coming and saying,
"yes, i'm ready for this."
because no matter what happens,

no matter who i meet,
i know that i am whole,
i am enough.
and i'll keep growing,
evolving,
and loving,
with every ounce of me.
i'll learn to let go of what no longer serves me,
i'll learn to trust the timing of my life,
i'll learn that not everything has to make sense right away.
sometimes the pieces fit together when they're meant to,
and other times, the puzzle is still being built.
but that's okay.
because in the meantime,
i'll keep living,
i'll keep breathing,
and i'll keep loving.
and when the right love comes along again,
i'll be ready to welcome it with open arms.
but i'll do it differently this time.
i'll do it with more patience,
more kindness,
more self-awareness.
because i've learned that love isn't about possession,
it's about sharing,
about growing together,
about supporting each other's dreams and desires,
without fear or hesitation.
i know now that love is not perfect,
but it is always worth it.
it's messy and beautiful,
complicated and simple,

WE AIN'T KIDS ANYMORE

all at the same time.
and i'm grateful for all the ways it has shaped me.
so, i look ahead with hope,
knowing that the best parts of me are still to come.
the love i have yet to give,
the dreams i have yet to chase,
the experiences i have yet to have.
i know they're out there,
waiting for me.
and in the meantime,
i'll cherish what i've learned,
i'll hold onto the memories,
and i'll keep loving myself,
in every way that i can.
because that's where it starts,
with loving myself first.
and so, with a heart full of gratitude,
i'll continue to walk forward.
i'll continue to live this life,
the way i was always meant to,
with love,
with joy,
with grace.
and i know that love, in whatever form it comes,
will always find me again.
and when it does,
i'll be ready.
and even on days when the weight of the world feels heavy,
when the doubts creep in and the past whispers in my ear,
i'll remember that i am not defined by the struggles,
by the heartbreaks,
by the things that didn't work out.

i am defined by how i rise,
by how i choose to keep going,
by how i choose to love,
even when it's hard.
because love, true love,
isn't about perfection.
it's about the moments of vulnerability,
of allowing yourself to be seen,
to be known,
to be raw.
and i know now,
more than ever,
that it's okay to not have everything figured out.
it's okay to still be learning,
to still be growing.
because growth is the essence of life,
and every step, no matter how small,
is progress.
so i'll take it one day at a time,
each step moving me closer to the person
i am becoming.
and even when i feel lost,
i'll remember that it's just a phase,
a part of the journey,
a moment in time that will pass.
because i know that i am resilient,
i am strong,
and i will keep moving forward.
and when the right love comes,
it won't feel like pressure.
it won't feel like a burden.
it will feel like a soft breeze,

WE AIN'T KIDS ANYMORE

a gentle pull,
a connection that flows effortlessly.
because love should feel like home,
like a place where you can rest,
be yourself,
and feel safe.
so i'll wait,
but i won't wait idly.
i'll live,
i'll chase my dreams,
i'll make the most of every moment.
and when that love finds me,
i'll be ready to give all of myself,
but only because i've learned to love myself first.
because the most important love,
the one that will carry me through anything,
is the love i have for me.
and once i've mastered that,
once i've built that foundation,
everything else will fall into place.
because love, at its core,
is a reflection of how we love ourselves.
so here's to the future,
to the unknown,
to all the beauty that's yet to unfold.
i'll embrace it all with open arms,
ready to learn,
ready to love,
ready to live.
and when i look back on all the days that led me here,
i'll smile,
knowing that every twist and turn,

every high and low,
was worth it.
because it brought me closer to this moment,
closer to understanding who i am,
who i want to be,
and what i want from this life.
so i'll keep walking forward,
i'll keep believing in the magic of the universe,
in the power of love,
and in the strength that comes from within.
i'll keep dreaming,
i'll keep hoping,
and i'll keep loving.
and when the right person walks into my life,
i'll be ready to build something beautiful,
something strong,
something that lasts.
but until then,
i'll be enough.
i'll be whole.
i'll be me.
i'll keep walking,
even when the path feels unclear,
because i know that clarity comes with time,
and i trust the rhythm of my journey.
the universe has its own way of guiding us,
and as long as i stay true to myself,
i know i'll end up exactly where i'm meant to be.
sometimes, it feels like the pieces don't fit,
like the dreams are just out of reach,
but i've learned that nothing is ever wasted.
every moment is a lesson,

every setback a stepping stone.
and with each step,
i'm becoming the person i've always wanted to be.
there's a beauty in the process,
in the messy moments when things don't go as planned.
because those are the moments that teach me who i am,
that shape me into someone who knows how to appreciate the good,
the small moments of joy,
the ones that make me stop and smile,
the ones that remind me that i'm alive.
and through it all,
i've learned that love isn't just about what you give to others,
it's about how you learn to give to yourself.
it's about the way you look in the mirror and say,
"i'm proud of you,"
even on the days when you feel small.
because self-love is the foundation of everything,
the root from which all other love grows.
and i'm learning to love myself in ways i never thought possible.
to appreciate my flaws,
to embrace my strengths,
to accept myself, even when i feel imperfect.
because i know now that i am worthy,
worthy of the love i give,
worthy of the dreams i chase,
worthy of every good thing that comes my way.
and when love comes knocking at my door again,
i'll welcome it with open arms,
but i won't lose myself in it.
i'll remember who i am,
who i've become,
and i'll give love freely,

without fear,
without hesitation.
because i know that love isn't about losing yourself,
it's about finding a new version of yourself,
one that grows alongside the other,
one that supports and encourages,
one that nurtures and thrives.
and i won't settle for anything less than that.
i'll only give my heart to someone who sees me,
who understands me,
who loves me for exactly who i am.
because i deserve that.
we all deserve that.
and as i continue this journey,
i'll remember to enjoy the little things.
the sunsets,
the quiet moments,
the laughter with friends,
the late-night talks,
the quiet peace of being with someone who gets it.
because those moments,
those are the ones that matter.
they are the ones that make life feel rich,
feel full.
and when i feel the weight of the world again,
when the doubts return,
when the fears rise up,
i'll take a deep breath and remember:
i am enough.
i am worthy.
i am loved.
and that's all that truly matters.

WE AIN'T KIDS ANYMORE

so here's to love—
to the love i give myself,
to the love i share with others,
to the love that is waiting for me in the future.
i'll keep moving forward,
with an open heart,
a mind full of dreams,
and a soul that's ready to embrace everything that comes my way.
because love is always worth it.
and i'll keep loving,
even when it feels hard,
because i know that in the end,
it's the love we give that makes life beautiful.
and i'm ready for all of it.
all the good,
all the bad,
all the love,
all the lessons.
because i know that no matter what,
i'll always be okay.
and that,
that is enough.
as i stand at the edge of the unknown,
i can feel the weight of everything that has come before,
the lessons learned, the heartaches felt,
the dreams built and then shattered,
the promises whispered into the dark
and the ones left unspoken.
it all leads here.
and yet, i can't help but wonder:
what happens next?
what comes after the silence?

when the final page is turned and the words fade away,
where do we go?
there's a stillness in the air now,
a quiet that speaks louder than any noise ever could,
a tension,
a holding of breath,
waiting for something—
something i can't yet see,
something i'm not yet ready for.
i've walked this path,
every step taking me closer to an answer,
or perhaps,
farther from it.
maybe the answer was never meant to be found,
maybe it was never in the destination,
but in the journey itself.
maybe i'll never know,
maybe i'll just keep walking,
moving,
breathing,
waiting for the moment when it all makes sense.
but even as i stand here,
looking out into the vast unknown,
i can't shake the feeling that something is just around the corner.
it's close now—
i can feel it in my bones,
in the pit of my stomach,
a whisper in the wind,
a shadow in the distance,
something i can't quite grasp,
but i know it's there.
and maybe,

WE AIN'T KIDS ANYMORE

just maybe,
the story isn't over yet.
maybe this is only the beginning.
because when you think you've reached the end,
when you believe there's nowhere else to go,
that's when the next chapter begins.
so i close this book,
but not with an ending,
but with a question.
and that question lingers—
a mystery i can't untangle,
but one i'm willing to live with.
what happens now?
where does this story go?
where do we go?
the only thing i know for sure is that I'm not done yet.
this isn't the last page.
this isn't the final word.
this is only the beginning of something greater,
something i can't even imagine yet.
and i'll keep writing,
keep dreaming,
keep believing.
because the story's not over—
it's just starting to unfold.
and whatever comes next,
whatever happens after all of this,
i'll be ready.
because i know now,
the ending is never truly the end.
it's just another beginning.

About the Author

Ceazia Barr is a passionate writer who finds inspiration in the intricacies of relationships, drawing from her own experiences and observations. Her debut novel reflects her talent for crafting emotionally resonant stories that explore love, pain, and the human spirit.

When Ceazia isn't writing, she enjoys spending time with her family, including her deeply loved mom, one sister, and two brothers. She's an avid player of The Sims 4 and adores watching videos of cats. Music is a constant source of joy for her, providing the perfect backdrop for her creative pursuits.

A true foodie at heart, Ceazia has a special love for street tacos, which she often enjoys during family gatherings. Through her writing, she hopes to connect with readers, spark meaningful conversations, and remind them that they're never alone in their struggles.

Ceazia's storytelling is a reflection of her passions, and her work is just the beginning of a journey that promises to touch hearts and inspire minds.